THE WORKING EXPERIENCE

TEACHER'S MANUAL

BY JEANNE H. SMITH AND HARRY RINGEL

New Readers Press

ISBN 0-88336-968-0

Copyright © 1991

 New Readers Press
Publishing Division of Laubach Literacy International
Box 131, Syracuse, New York 13210-0131

Printed in the United States of America

Sponsoring Editor: Paula Schlusberg
Manuscript Editor: Jeanna H. Walsh
Additional Editorial: Elizabeth Costello
Book Design: Kathleen T. Bates
Production: Mark Legler
Cover Design: WD Burdick Company

9 8 7 6 5 4 3 2

Table of Contents

Introduction

Book 1

Book 2

Book 3

Introduction

Purpose

The Working Experience is a series of texts designed for English as a Second Language (ESL) students. The series builds on oral skills to develop reading and writing ability while still expanding oral English-language proficiency. Thus, *The Working Experience* is particularly appropriate to the needs of an ever-growing segment of the ESL population: students whose speaking and listening skills in English far surpass their ability to read and write the language. Because of its emphasis on the *integration* of language skills, however, the series can benefit almost any student engaged in learning English.

One of the basic principles underlying *The Working Experience* is the conviction that students learn best when the content relates to their daily lives. Therefore, while working through this series of thematically coordinated texts, students read about, talk about, and sometimes write about issues they confront every day. The words and concepts introduced have immediate importance, and students are given the opportunity to practice and ultimately internalize what they've learned in all language areas. The readings and exercises that make up *The Working Experience* allow students to share meaningful learning experiences in a flexible, multilevel format.

Overview of the Series

Work is an issue of interest and importance to most adults. To adults of limited English proficiency, it can be an even more vital and confounding aspect of life in what is for many of them not only a new job but also a new land. It is for this reason that *The Working Experience* uses as its basic text stories told by other adult ESL students. These stories all relate in some fashion to the narrators' work experiences in either this country or their native lands. Your ESL students will have an opportunity to read about the experiences of people who are in some ways like themselves, and thus can identify with the story-tellers because of shared experiences expressed in a commonly new language.

The components

The Working Experience consists of three student texts as well as this teacher's manual. Each student text contains 15 short readings followed by exercises related to the reading. The teacher's manual provides an introduction to the series, suggestions for working through the lessons, and lesson notes and exercise answers for all three student books.

The readings

The student texts, Books 1, 2, and 3, are not tied to traditional "reading levels," but reading difficulty does increase from book to book. It should be noted, however, that the readings are sequenced only in this broadest sense. A student need not complete Book 1 before moving on to Book 2, nor do the lessons within each book need to be completed in order.

Essentially, Book 1 targets a "high beginning" reading level. Students will most likely have at least heard the words they will be asked to read and write. The reading passages involve straightforward declarative sentence structures and simple verb tenses. In Book 2, the readings challenge students with greater variety in verb tense and sentence structure. The longer readings in Book 3 employ more complex sentence structures, and the content is more abstract.

The exercises

Like the readings, the exercises increase in difficulty and demand more of students from book to book. *The Working Experience* features a variety of exercises; some are text-based, some elicit conversation, and others focus on a particular grammatical structure or on vocabulary development. It should be noted that the grammar exercises do not build on each other from lesson to lesson. Rather, they are of a "troubleshooting" nature and are inspired by the text they accompany. Their purpose is to practice and reinforce key structures which students have been exposed to in the reading passages.

Every lesson in the student books ends with an opportunity for personal expression. Students can work on this exercise independently, or you may wish to engage them in a Language Experience Activity (LEA). Background information on the Language Experience approach and suggestions for leading your own LEA are discussed in the section below.

Using Language Experience

In general, the Language Experience approach utilizes students' own words as the basis for readings and exercises. As a student tells a story, the instructor writes down what is being said. Then the story is written out or typed and becomes the "text" for a subsequent lesson.

Language Experience is widely used for developing literacy skills among native English speakers. For ESL students, the pedagogy takes on both added benefits and obstacles. Participating in an LEA can build students' speaking skills while also encouraging vocabulary enrichment to meet their own needs. In addition, an LEA increases students' confidence by using familiar topics and the students' own words to create a written text. Using the strategy outlined below can help make an LEA a pleasant, productive exercise for you and your students.

Keep in mind that an LEA works equally well with individuals, small groups, and larger classes. One of the most successful and accessible LEA applications involves getting a whole class to contribute to an LEA that you write on the blackboard.

How do I get started?

Each lesson in the student texts ends with "What's Your Story?," a suggested topic for an LEA exercise that is thematically related to the content of the reading passage. If your students, for any reason, cannot respond to the topic in the text, you'll find alternative topics listed in the lesson notes section of this manual. Once you've chosen a topic, begin the LEA by prompting students with simple and specific questions related to the topic. These questions are your "story starters." Story starters are crucial to an LEA because they start students talking and keep the process going.

As students respond to the story starters, jot down their remarks. Help students when they falter: don't panic at pauses, and don't worry about getting every word down exactly.

Where should the story go?

The story may be about anything. It might develop out of the theme of the textbook reading, or it might leave it entirely behind. For example, one student may respond to reading a "first job" story in the text with complaints about the difficulties in filling out an application form. If this happens with it; let the students' interests be your guide. The important thing get students involved in an LEA, and the best way to do this is to work with topics the students find meaningful.

With beginning students, you'll find it is most productive to stick to fairly concrete discussions of their own experiences. As students gain more control over their new language, they can move beyond their own experiences, and they will want to include more opinion, evaluation, inference, and speculation in their stories.

The LEA story can be as long or short as students like. For beginners, a few sentences may be enough. For more advanced students, try to stay within a page to keep your lesson manageable. If you think you have enough for a story, even after just a few lines, ask students whether they have anything else to add. If they do not, feel free to stop.

Where do I go from here?

Once you have an LEA story to work with, you can develop follow-up exercises to reinforce learning. You can use the exercise formats already found in the student texts: true/false, fill-in, cloze, vocabulary review, writing practice, number work, word families, sentence completion, and grammar activities of various sorts. In developing exercises, vary them as much as possible to cover the four basics of any ESL lesson: reading, writing, listening, and speaking. Try to include activities that focus on both content comprehension and language analysis, but keep exercises simple. Once you're acquainted with a variety of patterns, you'll find you can quickly develop effective exercises.

What should I watch out for?

When you're doing an LEA with ESL students, two problems are likely to arise. First, there is the question of what to do with incomplete or nonstandard structures that students use as they are speaking. Do not dwell on them. You can edit student stories without violating their spirit. Students appreciate seeing their own words on paper and will be happy to read your structural reworkings of language errors they generally won't know they've made. Remember that exploring language is the goal of an LEA for ESL students. Focusing too much on language problems can weaken the activity.

A second problem involves vocabulary limitations. Students will often grope for language as they tell a story. When they do so, be patient. In group or classroom LEAs, let students confer with each other or use dictionaries to build the story. Help them find words; after all, discussing words is conversation, too. Look upon this process as an opportunity for language growth.

LEAs allow learning to proceed from a student-centered base, rather than a textbook-centered one. As long as your students are willing to talk and you are willing to listen, LEAs will continue to generate new lessons and learning will happen.

 ## Facilitating Reading

Each one of the lessons in *The Working Experience* contains a reading passage. If your students have had minimal exposure to printed English, you may choose to read the passage aloud while students follow along in their books. Keep in mind that the purpose in reading aloud is not only to read so students can hear a story or obtain information, but also to help students to simultaneously see, hear, and understand the written passage.

You may wish to try out some of the oral and silent reading techniques outlined below. They often help to enhance comprehension. These techniques by no means exhaust the possibilities for oral and silent reading, but are sufficient to inject some variety into the reading segment of the lessons. You may also wish to create your own adaptations of these techniques.

Oral reading

At all levels of ESL instruction, oral reading can be useful because the practice in pronunciation and speaking it provides can increase students' ability and confidence with independent conversational English. Furthermore, students enjoy the oral reading because they can hear themselves speak and pronounce English words. Oral reading can be helpful for you, too, as it will let you know if and when students need assistance with pronunciation, or whether they are familiar with particular words.

In both group and one-on-one settings, you can help students get used to reading aloud by using the echo reading or duet reading methods. These methods, which are described below, also aid in comprehension because they move the student from focusing on the meaning of individual words to understanding the meanings of phrases, sentences, and paragraphs.

- **Echo reading**
  In this technique, students repeat phrases or sentences after you read them aloud. You can stop at the end of a line, phrase, or sentence to let students repeat the words. If, however, stopping at the end of a line will break a flow in meaning, it is best to stop before the line ends or else

continue to the next line so that the message being conveyed is complete. Students can also practice echo reading on their own by working with a recording of the story.

- **Duet reading**

  This technique is a combination of reading aloud and echo reading. In duet reading, students read aloud with you. Sometimes you'll read just a little bit ahead of the students, almost finishing the pronunciation of a single, whole, unknown word before they attempt to read it. Other times, when students are familiar with particular words, you can let them read independently. Duet reading is useful because it gives students an opportunity to get some assistance without relying totally on you to read for them. A lot of practice with the duet reading method can successfully facilitate students' eventual reading independence.

Silent reading

As students become more independent users, readers, and speakers of English, they will be confronted with situations where oral reading is not comfortable or appropriate. For example, reading a job application form in a personnel office and reading handouts at a parents' meeting are just two situations where silent reading is more appropriate.

You can be of great help to students as they make the transition from oral to silent reading. Directed reading and retelling activities, briefly described below, are useful techniques for this purpose.

- **Directed reading**

  Directed reading involves asking students to read to find the answers to specific questions. Questions create a purpose for reading; when students focus on the meaning of what they are reading rather than how the words sound when read aloud, they move from saying the words to "thinking" the words. In ESL instruction, directed reading also becomes speaking practice because students answer the questions orally, and their answers can lead to further discussion.

  One option in directing silent reading is to create predictive questions based on a story title and then ask students to read the story to find the answers. You can also pick two or three elements of the story (significant events, facts, etc.), create a question about each one, and ask students to read to find the answers. These questions can be written on the board or on a piece of paper that is distributed to the class.

  Students can read an entire passage before discussing the answers to these questions, or they can read only until they find an answer and then discuss that answer before continuing.

Story scanning is another option. This activity can be used to focus students' attention during an initial reading, or it can provide follow-up review of a story. Students are instructed to scan a story quickly and find all the instances of a particular category of words. Story scanning can focus on a language feature (e.g., all the words that end in *-ing* or words, abbreviations, and initials that begin with capital letters) or on a semantic category (e.g., all the words for food, all the words relating to job hunting, or all the names of job benefits mentioned in a story).

- **Retelling**

  Another, more open-ended silent reading activity is to have students retell what they read during their silent reading. Retelling gives students a chance to articulate their understanding of what they read and then, of course, to re-read to check for details they may have missed. Retelling can be easily used with stories from *The Working Experience* and can be useful at all levels.

 ## Teaching the Lesson

Each lesson in the student books adheres to the same basic structure. The lesson begins with preview/pre-reading activities, followed by the reading of the passage around which the lesson is centered. The reading is followed by exercises geared toward comprehension, language skills, and discussion, culminating in a writing activity.

The comprehension exercises are, of course, related to the reading and come in a variety of formats: true/false, complete the sentence, fill-in, multiple choice, etc. The language skills exercises are also inspired by the reading passage, but deal in general with grammar patterns, sentence structure, and vocabulary review and expansion. The discussion questions fall under the rubric "Follow-up" and are focused on both literal issues and opinion or evaluation activities. Finally, each follow-up section ends with an activity called "What's Your Story?," which can be a lead-in to a group or individual LEA.

Below you'll find suggestions for handling the pre-reading and reading sections, as well as descriptions of the kinds of exercises that appear in *The Working Experience*.

Pre-reading

Pre-reading is a vital step in the ESL learning process. It prepares students for the different aspects of a lesson before the reading is even considered. The lessons in *The Working Experience* lend themselves to three types of pre-reading: discussion preview, picture preview, and word preview.

- **Discussion preview**

  Discussion preview aims at getting students acquainted with and thinking about the themes that will be brought up by the reading passage. Of course, students may already have experience with these themes. Discussion preview is a good opportunity to elicit this background information and allow students to share their knowledge with each other. In addition, you can use this time to fill in any gaps in their background and to introduce relevant concepts. The discussion should also provide an opportunity to elicit or introduce much of the key vocabulary that students will encounter in the story.

  One good way to start a discussion preview is to ask students to reply to the "lead question" in the text. You'll find this question at the top of the first page of each lesson. The lesson notes list additional questions and guidelines for conducting a discussion about other elements of the story. Keep in mind that these discussions need not be very involved or too detailed. Students can deal with the topic in greater detail during the follow-up discussion and LEA portions of the lesson.

- **Picture preview**

  Every reading passage in *The Working Experience* is preceded by a photograph that relates to the content or theme of the story. Discussing this picture with students is another good pre-reading activity. Like discussion preview, picture preview is a way to draw on students' knowledge of English and the world while preparing them for reading the story. It's an additional chance to highlight key concepts and vocabulary students will encounter in the reading.

  The pictures are not meant to be illustrations of the people or places described in the story. Rather, they are a visual expression of some aspect of the story's theme. The lesson notes provide suggested questions or guidelines to stimulate discussion of each picture. When students discuss the picture, it's often enough for them to simply describe what they see. But as their language skills develop, you'll want to encourage them to offer opinions about the picture and even make speculations about its content. The important thing is for students to relate what's in the picture to their own lives as often as possible.

- **Word preview**

  Word preview is a very important type of pre-reading exercise, especially for ESL students. The object of word preview activities is to familiarize students with some of the more difficult words in the reading passage before they actually attempt to read it. This way, students are better able to read for content, as opposed to plodding from one unknown word to the next.

There are several ways to approach word preview. One option is to focus on vocabulary. Choose words that are likely to be difficult for students, or that are essential to understanding the story. Ideally, most of these words will come up in the discussion preview or picture preview. If they don't, be sure to go over them with students before they begin to read.

Sight words present another word preview opportunity. Common words students are likely to encounter and to use in many contexts outside the classroom can be put on flash cards and reviewed periodically. Students will develop a "bank" of sight words that relate to their daily lives as well as to work situations.

If you wish, you can do word preview by focusing on sound-spelling correspondences and pronunciation patterns with which students are likely to have trouble.

Specific guidelines for word preview activities have not been included in the lesson notes. You will want to gear this part of the preview to meet your students' specific needs, using vocabulary or pronunciation techniques that you find most useful.

Reading the stories

Once you've completed the pre-reading activities, students will be eager to start reading. We recommend using a variety of oral and silent reading techniques. You can choose appropriate techniques from the section called "Facilitating Reading" on page 11.

Doing the exercises

The exercises in *The Working Experience* begin by focusing on meaning. Initial comprehension exercises give students the opportunity to understand the story as a whole. The language skills exercises that follow then direct students to look at the meanings, structures, and connections of individual words, phrases, and sentences. The follow-up exercises bring students back again to the story as a whole, creating opportunities for them to again think about the message in the story. The different types of exercises that appear in *The Working Experience* are outlined below.

- **Comprehension**
  Comprehension exercises in *The Working Experience* consist largely of true/false exercises, fill-ins, and complete-the-sentence activities.

True/false questions are used throughout the series because they encourage students to think about, recall, and clarify their understanding of what was read. The fill-in and complete-the-sentence activities ask students to read the story again and fill in the blanks with the correct words. These exercises are used because they show students the contextual value of words. By choosing the correct word or phrase to fill in a blank, students focus on what makes sense in a group of words. Fill-in exercises give a word bank that contains possible answers for the activity. Complete-the-sentence exercises do not provide this word bank. Students need to refer back to the story or supply the answer from memory. In these exercises, students may supply a word or phrase which does not match the reading passage but which still fits the meaning and structure of the sentence. Use this as an opportunity to teach how different words can and do make sense in the same sentence.

As the lessons progress, some comprehension exercises include multiple choice sentence completion and applying ordering/time sequencing. These exercises require that students have a broader grasp of the story. They need to deal with the story as a whole rather than focusing on specific details.

- **Language Skills**

The language skills exercises in *The Working Experience* provide additional practice in many of the rich and varied structures and vocabulary of the English language. All the activities are rooted in the language which is used in the actual stories. An overview of the types of exercises appears below.

Vocabulary Review. Students study the meaning of new words from the story in varied ways. They may be asked to match words with associated meanings, such as a job to a workplace or an activity to who does the activity. Some exercises ask students to complete sentences with new words they have learned. Many exercises ask students to circle the correct word from a choice of two words, so that the correct word completes a sentence about the story. Other exercises focus on synonyms, antonyms, and abbreviations.

Word Families. These exercises focus on the formation of new words by adding prefixes and/or suffixes. Students learn to recognize the way in which adding a prefix or suffix to a root word changes its part of speech, to see the meaning relationship between the root word and the new word, and to develop a sense of which form they should use in different sentence structures.

Number Work. When stories include the discussion of numbers or money, some number work activities may follow. These are designed to help students internalize the relationship between numbers and words for practical use.

Capital Letters. Capital letters instruction focuses on using capital letters to begin sentences and to begin names of people, places, holidays, and days of the week. Exercises progress from writing single letters to writing whole words.

Structure Practice. Structure practice exercises introduce the student to some basic structural considerations for standard English. The scope of these exercises is not meant to be all-inclusive, nor is it intended as a full-scale grammar curriculum. Although some parts of speech are mentioned, learning terms and rules is not the focus. The goal is to help students become aware of some of the basic elements of sentence construction and language use through activities which expand on the English used in the stories.

The structure practice exercises address key areas that ESL students need to master, including singular/plural forms, verb tenses, prepositions, possessives, sentence combining, subordinate clauses, pronoun forms, and contractions.

- **Follow-up**

  Let's Talk about It. This exercise appears throughout the series and consists of questions about the story that students can read and then answer out loud. The questions may be literal or inferential, and students can look back at the story if they need to. In some cases, answers will vary, though, depending on students' backgrounds and opinions. Answering the questions out loud will give students additional practice with spoken English, and may lead to further discussion.

  A Closer Look. These activities focus on specific words or elements from the story, and students are asked to use knowledge from their own lives to expand on these concepts. For example, if a story talks about joining a union, students are asked to take a closer look at what a union does by sharing what they know about unions and their function. A Closer Look activities also focus on understanding pronouns and reference items.

  Thinking about the Story. There is more to understand about a story than what the words actually say. In this activity, students focus on one aspect or theme of the story and discuss or analyze it, based on their own knowledge and experience. For example, they might examine causes of prejudice or explore their views of what a good worker is like.

  A good way to conduct this activity is to have students work in pairs or small groups. They can discuss both sides of an issue, offer opinions, share information, clarify ideas, and pose solutions to problems. Then these small groups can report back to the larger class. These activities can, if you wish, lead to individual or group writing activities, as well.

What's Your Story? Many students will have had direct or indirect experiences similar to the ones they read about in *The Working Experience*. What's Your Story? gives the students an opportunity to share their own accounts of comparable situations and can function as a lead-in to a group or individual LEA. The LEA method, as described in "Using Language Experience" on page 9, is highly recommended as a means to record student stories, particularly for students working in Book 1.

There are many ways to use student responses to this activity. If you wish, compile these stories and save them for further reading practice. Students can read their stories aloud to one another, and may also want to keep a collection of their stories in a journal.

If, for any reason, your students cannot respond to the topic presented in the student text, alternative topics are provided in the lesson notes.

 ## Using the Series in Multilevel Classrooms

The Working Experience is designed for use in a variety of educational settings. Its intended audience is adult and teen-aged ESL students in large classes, small groups, or one-on-one tutorials. The series can be used on its own or in conjunction with other texts and, while it is not a vocational or pre-vocational series, it can be useful in those contexts as well.

Many ESL classrooms cater to students with disparate levels of English-language ability. *The Working Experience* is easily adapted to serve the needs of a multilevel classroom. Lessons with corresponding themes appear in all three textbooks. Therefore, you can begin by discussing a common theme with the group as a whole, and then let students work through a lesson on that theme at their own level. A unit about "My First Job," for example, might begin with a preview discussion in which the whole class participates. After the discussion, each student can work through a lesson on this theme in whichever book is most appropriate. Students can then come back together as a group for the follow-up discussion and LEA.

Book 1

The Working Experience Lesson Notes

1 My Father's Store
Soo Lim

Discussion Preview

1. Suggested questions: What is a grocery store? What (in general) do you buy in a grocery store? Make a list of these things on the board. Ask students to explain new words to each other. Use pictures to help explain unfamiliar products.

2. Ask students to describe neighborhood stores where they shop. Suggested questions: What does the store sell? What do they buy in the store? Who shops there? Who works in the store? What does the outside or inside of the store look like?

Picture Preview

Who is the man in the picture? or What does he do? Where is he working? What does he sell in his store? Does he look happy? Do you think he likes his work? Why or why not?

Comprehension

- **True or False**
  1. F   2. F   3. F   4. T   5. T   6. F

- **Fill-in**
  1. small   4. good
  2. old   5. black
  3. many   6. play

Language Skills

- **Vocabulary Review**
  1. shop
  2. neighborhood
  3. sandwich
  4. candy
  5. customers

- **Structure Practice**
  1. *Soo's father*
  2. customer's sandwich
  3. child's candy
  4. neighbor's groceries
  5. family's store

- **Word Families**
  1. Asia
  2. Korean
  3. America
  4. Asian
  5. Korea
  6. American

  This exercise illustrates only one pattern for making a modifier or language from a name of a country or continent. For additional practice: Colombia–Colombian, Russia–Russian, Puerto Rico–Puerto Rican, Cambodia–Cambodian. Your students' nationalities may provide other examples.

- **Number Work**

  Be sure students know the meaning of the ¢ symbol and know that it is equivalent to the word *cent(s)*.

  penny—1¢   dime—10¢
  nickel—5¢   quarter—25¢

Follow-up

- **Let's Talk about It**
  1. in her father's store
  2. in a very old neighborhood in the city
  3. black people, Asian people, Korean people, children
  4. because the sandwiches are good, because they sell groceries, because customers can buy Korean and American food
  5. because they buy candy there, because they stay and play in the store

- **What's Your Story?**
  Alternative topics: Tell about the place where someone you know works. Tell about a grocery store or neighborhood store where you shop. (Refer to Discussion Preview #2.)

2 The Boss
Josefina Rivera

Discussion Preview

1. Discuss with students what they know about factories and factory work. Ask them what kinds of jobs people have in factories. Ask if they think those are good jobs or not.
2. Discuss who and what a boss is. Discuss what a boss does. Ask them what a good boss is like and what a bad boss is like. They can describe the behavior of both types or list the characteristics.

Picture Preview

1. Ask students to describe the man in the picture. Encourage them to guess about his personality. Suggested questions: Does he look like a pleasant man? Does he look happy? sad? angry? nice? mean? Do you want to know this man?
2. What do you think the man does? Do you think he is a nice man to work for? How do you think he behaves with people who work for him? Would you like to work for him?

Comprehension

- **True or False**
  1. F   2. T   3. T   4. T   5. F   6. F
- **Complete the Sentence**
  1. *factory*   4. scream
  2. respect   5. jobs
  3. equally   6. money

Language Skills

- **Vocabulary Review**
  1. talk
  2. hard
  3. money
  4. factory
  5. respect

- **Word Families**

  work—worker

  bake—baker

  paint—painter

  drive—driver

  teach—teacher

  For more practice: read–reader, shop–shopper, speak–speaker, write–writer, manage–manager. Students may have examples of their own, related to their jobs.

- **Singular and Plural**
  1. jobs
  2. workers
  3. teachers
  4. students
  5. cars

Follow-up

- **Let's Talk about It**

  The answers here express Josefina's opinions. Students' opinions will vary.

  1. bosses
  2. workers
  3. bosses
  4. They don't respect them; they don't treat them equally; they scream; they talk nasty.
  5. She does not like the bosses in factories.

- **What's Your Story?**

  Alternative topics: Tell about a boss you had in the past or one you know about (e.g., a friend's boss). Discuss what makes a boss good or bad, in general.

3 Day Off
Ligia Figueroa

Discussion Preview

1. Discuss the term *day off*. Suggested questions: Do you work or go to your job every day? How many days do you work? On which days don't you work? What do you call the days when you don't work?

2. How many days make up the work week in your native country? How many days off do most people have in your native country?

Picture Preview

Ask what the woman is doing. Get students to say (at least), "She is cooking (dinner); she is looking around the room/apartment." Ask students to make some guesses. What is she thinking about? What else does she want to do (in her apartment)?

Comprehension

- **True or False**
  1. T   2. T   3. F   4. F   5. T   6. F

- **Complete the Sentence**

1. day	5. cook
2. clean	6. shopping
3. wash	7. stores
4. sit, coffee	8. lunch

Language Skills

- **Vocabulary Review**

1. look	4. drink, watch
2. clean	5. look
3. wash	

- **Capital Letters: Beginning Sentences**
  1. *O*   2. T   3. S   4. W   5. W

- **Structure Practice**
  wash—the clothes
  clean—the house
  watch—television
  eat—lunch
  go—shopping

Follow-up

- **Let's Talk about It**
  1. looks around her house, cleans her house
  2. the clothes
  3. Answers will vary. Encourage students to make guesses.
  4. her sister
  5. at a nice restaurant
  6. Answers will vary.

- **What's Your Story?**
  Alternative topics: What do people in your native country do on a day off? What do you do to have fun?

 My First Job
Alberta Henderson

Discussion Preview

How many people do you work with? Do you all have the same job or different ones? Do you like those people?

Picture Preview

1. Suggested questions: What are the people in the picture doing? What place do you think they are working in? What do you think they are making? What is the name of the machine they are using?
2. Does this look like a pleasant place to work? How do you think the people in the picture feel about their work?

Comprehension

- **True or False**
  1. F 2. T 3. T 4. F 5. F 6. T

- **Complete the Sentence**

  1. name
  2. clothing
  3. sewing
  4. sew
  5. workers
  6. same
  7. think

Language Skills

- **Structure Practice: Singular and Plural**

  1. hems
  2. seams
  3. workers
  4. linings
  5. jobs
  6. machines

- **Capital Letters: Names of People**

  The answers will be different for each student.

- **Structure Practice: Present Tense**

  work, makes, use, is, think, make

Follow-up

- **Let's Talk about It**

  1. in a clothing factory
  2. 40 or 50
  3. She sews, makes stitches, sews linings, and finishes hems and seams (or other variations).
  4. yes
  5. Answers will vary. Students can discuss whether Alberta's work is easy or difficult, interesting or boring. They may also note that she says she gets along with the other workers.

- **What's Your Story?**

  Alternative topics: Do you know someone who has a good job? Tell about that person's job and why it is good.

Women's Work
Pilar Duyer

Discussion Preview

Ask students if women work outside the home in their country. What do they do? Compare and contrast the responses about different countries.

Picture Preview

1. What is this woman doing? What is the name of her job? What is the name of the place where she works? If necessary, discuss the differences between the terms *beautician* (or *hairdresser*) and *barber,* between *beauty shop* and *barber shop*.

2. Do women in your native country cut men's hair? Do men there go to beauty shops?

Comprehension

- **True or False**
  1. T   2. T   3. F   4. T   5. F

- **Complete the Sentence**
  1. women   4. factory
  2. different   5. jobs
  3. beauty   6. benefits

Language Skills

- **Vocabulary Review**
  nurse—hospital
  waitress—restaurant
  beautician—beauty shop
  saleswoman—store

- **Word Families**
  1. beautician   4. wait
  2. waitress   5. beautiful
  3. beauty

- **Structure Practice**
  They are nurses, beauticians, saleswomen, and waitresses.
  They work in restaurants, in stores, in hospitals, in beauty shops, and in factories.

Follow-up

- **Let's Talk about It**
  1. in restaurants, stores, hospitals, beauty shops, factories
  2. They work as waitresses, saleswomen, nurses, beauticians, factory workers.

3. They do the same jobs as women in other parts of the United States.

4. women in Puerto Rico

5. women in Puerto Rico

6. Answers will vary. Possible answers: teacher, business owner, doctor, politician, secretary, cab or bus driver, or computer programmer.

- **What's Your Story?**
  Alternative topics: Tell about the jobs men do in your native country. Compare the jobs women do in your native country and the United States, or some other country. (Refer to Discussion Preview.)

6 Money
Maria Velasquez

Discussion Preview

1. Ask students to name the different ways that workers can get paid for a job. Elicit phrases such as "by check" or "in cash." Find out how students have been paid in the past. Ask how most people are paid in students' native countries.

2. Discuss the word *benefits*. List different kinds of benefits workers can get in America and/or students' native countries. Discuss which benefits students think are most important.

Picture Preview

1. Use the picture to elicit key vocabulary from the story. Ask students to identify what they see: money/bills/coins, glasses, medicine/pills/prescription medicine/pill bottles.

2. Ask students if their job benefits include glasses or medicine. Discuss what benefits they do get at their jobs.

Comprehension

- **True or False**
  1. T   2. T   3. F   4. T   5. T   6. F
- **Fill-in**

  1. check   4. pay
  2. makes   5. rate
  3. benefits   6. taxes

Language Skills

- **Vocabulary Review**
  1. prescription
  2. taxes
  3. company
  4. check
  5. salary

- **Word Families**
  1. prescription
  2. medical
  3. prescribe
  4. medicine
  5. prescription

- **Same Sound, Different Word**
  1. too
  2. to
  3. their
  4. two
  5. there
  6. too

- **Structure Practice: Verbs**
  gets, pays, loses, hopes, gets

Follow-up

- **Let's Talk about It**
  1. $4.25 per hour
  2. by check
  3. prescription medicine and glasses
  4. $80 a month
  5. Her salary is too low; she pays too much for benefits and taxes.
  6. Possible answers: Maria will want a higher salary, periodic raises, more benefits, and perhaps also better benefits.

- **What's Your Story?**
  Alternative topics: What benefits do you get in your job? What benefits are important for workers, and why? (Refer to Discussion Preview #2.)

 7 ## A Hard Part of My Job
Chantha Nou

Discussion Preview

1. If students work, ask them to tell what the hardest part of their job is.

2. Ask students what they think is the most difficult cleaning activity for them when they have to be housekeepers, as we all do. Discuss the responses.

Picture Preview

1. Use the picture to elicit discussion of a housekeeper's job and the vocabulary related to that job. Suggested questions: What is she doing? Where do you think she is working? What room is she cleaning? What else will she clean in that room? What else do you think she does in her job? What is her job called? Students may call her job *maid*. Present the term *housekeeper* if students do not mention it.

2. Ask students if they think the woman likes her job, if they think it is a good job, if they think it is a difficult or an easy job.

Comprehension

- **True or False**
  1. F   2. F   3. F   4. T

- **Complete the Sentence**
  1. housekeeper   4. inspects
  2. mirrors   5. complains
  3. time (to finish the job)

Language Skills

- **Vocabulary Review**
  1. complains   3. clean
  2. finish   4. activity

- **Compound Words**

  some times   store keeper
  work day   sales woman
  house keeper

- **Fill-in**
  1. uncleaned   4. unemployed
  2. unopened   5. unpaid
  3. undressed

  Examples for further practice: unhappy, unofficial, unmarried

- **Structure Practice**

  1. this   4. these

  2. these   5. these

  3. this   6. this

Follow-up

- **Let's Talk about It**

  1. She is a housekeeper for a family. She cleans rooms.

  2. because it is hard for her to reach the mirrors to clean them

  3. because sometimes the mirrors are not clean, because sometimes Chantha doesn't finish her job and leaves mirrors uncleaned

  4. because the mirrors are too high, because she doesn't have enough time to finish her work

  5. Answers will vary.

- **What's Your Story?**

  Alternative topic: What is a difficult activity that you do around your home? Examples: repairing something, working in the garden, cleaning something, etc.

8 My Job
Priti Vyas

Discussion Preview

1. Make sure students understand what a sample is. Suggested questions: Do you ever get free samples of things in the mail or in a store? What kinds of samples do you get? Why do you get these samples? Why do you think clothing makers make samples of clothes?

2. What are some of the jobs in a clothing factory? What are some of the steps in making clothing?

Picture Preview

What is the woman in the picture doing? Where do you think she is working? What do you think she might be making? Encourage students to make guesses.

Comprehension

- **True or False**

  1. T   2. F   3. T   4. F   5. T   6. T   7. F

- **Complete the Sentence**

  1. sample
  2. clothes
  3. fabric
  4. fabric
  5. supervisor's
  6. department
  7. fun

Language Skills

- **Vocabulary Review**

  1. sample
  2. pieces
  3. garment
  4. nature
  5. fun
  6. week
  7. day

- **Structure Practice**

  1. *supervisor's name*
  2. children's toys
  3. manager's office
  4. Yvonne's mother
  5. son's teacher

- **Number Work**

  1. *eight—8*
  2. seven—7
  3. eight—8
  4. five—5

  Answer for yourself: Answers will vary.

Follow-up

- **Let's Talk about It**

  1. in a sample room
  2. in a clothing factory
  3. Alma
  4. She sews the cut pieces together to make a finished garment.

5. five days a week, eight hours a day

6. because she has a good nature

7. because her supervisor has a good nature, because she likes the people in her department, because her job is fun

- **What's Your Story?**

  Alternative topics: Tell about a job you want or that you think is fun to do. Tell about your supervisor.

9 How I Got My Job
Yvonne Largaespada

Discussion Preview

Do people get jobs in America if they don't know English? What kinds of jobs can they get?

Picture Preview

Ask students what the woman in the picture is looking at. If they can't identify it, explain that she is looking at Help Wanted signs, or advertisements for jobs. Ask if they think this is a good way to find a job. Ask if they have seen signs or ads like the one in the picture in the United States.

Comprehension

- **True or False**

  1. F   2. T   3. T   4. F   5. T   6. F   7. F

- **Complete the Sentence**

  1. Yvonne
  2. the United States
  3. months
  4. get a job
  5. mother
  6. factory
  7. supervisors

Language Skills

- **Structure Practice: Past Tense**

  1. *start*
  2. want
  3. talk
  4. work
  5. help
  6. ask

- **Fill-in**

  helped, asked, talked, wanted, started

- **Structure Practice**

  1. I really wanted to work, but I didn't know English.

  2. My mother talked to her supervisors, and they gave me a job.

Follow-up

- **Let's Talk about It**

  1. Nicaragua

  2. a few months ago (or, a short time ago)

  3. She really wanted to get a job.

  4. She didn't know English.

  5. her mother's supervisors

  6. her mother

- **What's Your Story?**

  Alternative topic: Tell about a person who you think will be able to help you find a job. Why will that person be able to help you?

10 **Respect**
Nilsa Rodriguez

Discussion Preview

1. Suggested questions: How does your boss behave toward you? What does your boss say about your work? What is the right way for a boss to treat a worker, in your opinion?

2. In your opinion, what is respect? What is respectful treatment or behavior? When have you been treated with respect? When have you not been treated with respect?

Picture Preview

What is the woman in the picture doing? Where is she working? Do you think she works hard? How many hours a day do you think she works? Is her pay good or not? Do you think she likes her job?

Comprehension

- **True or False**

  1. F   2. F   3. T   4. F   5. F   6. F

- **Complete the Sentence**

  1. restaurant   4. criticized

  2. hours   5. disrespectful

  3. owner   6. respect

Language Skills

- **Capital Letters: Days of the Week**

  Sunday, Monday, Tuesday, Wednesday, Thursday, Friday, Saturday

- **Same Sound, Different Word**

  1. to   5. two

  2. two   6. to

  3. too   7. to

  4. too

- **Word Families**

  1. criticized   4. critical

  2. respectful   5. respect

  3. disrespect

Follow-up

- **Let's Talk about It**

  1. 18

  2. 10 hours a day from Monday through Saturday

  3. He treated her with disrespect. He criticized everything she did. He wanted her to work more hours for the same pay.

  4. work more hours for the same pay

  5. She told him that he had to treat her with respect. Otherwise, she would not stay.

  6. Answers will vary. Possible answers: Nilsa felt unhappy or angry; she wanted to be treated with respect.

  7. Answers will vary.

- **What's Your Story?**

  Alternative topics: Do you know a boss who treats workers with respect? Tell about a situation in which someone showed respect for you.

11 Take-home Pay
Margarita Vemba

Discussion Preview

Ask students to list what a company can deduct from a paycheck. Have them group the deductions in two categories: required (e.g., social security, taxes) and optional (e.g., health insurance, Christmas Club).

Picture Preview

1. Ask students to identify what they see in the picture. Point to the calendar; ask how often they get paid and whether they are always paid on the same day of the week or month (e.g., every Friday). Do they have Blue Cross or some other health insurance? Does the company pay for it, or does the company deduct money from the paychecks?

2. The savings book can symbolize banks, and the students can discuss what a person does at a bank, or what services a bank offers.

3. The box of handkerchiefs relates directly to the story. You can also bring in a handkerchief to show students, and demonstrate the word *fold*, which will be used in the story.

Comprehension

- **True or False**
  1. F   2. T   3. T   4. F   5. T   6. F

Language Skills

- **Vocabulary Review**
  1. check
  2. social security
  3. taxes
  4. salary
  5. income
  6. deduct

- **Structure Practice**
  1. $10.00 per person
  2. two weeks per year
  3. three times per day
  4. $10.95 per person
  5. $49.00 per night
  6. 55 miles per hour

- **Capital Letters: Holidays**
  1. Thanksgiving
  2. President's Day
  3. Independence Day
  4. New Year's Eve
  5. Halloween
  6. Labor Day

- **Number Work**

1. *25 cents*	*$.25*	25¢
2. 75 cents	$.75	75¢
3. 12 cents	$.12	*12¢*
4. *52 cents*	$.52	52¢
5. 2 cents	*$.02*	2¢

Follow-up

- **Let's Talk about It**
  1. because she has friends where she works
  2. She works at the machine that folds the handkerchiefs.
  3. $4.70
  4. every week, every Friday
  5. no, only people who want to get it
  6. nothing

- **What's Your Story?**
  Alternative topic: How can/do you save money for Christmas or birthday presents or for other celebrations?

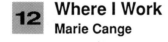

Where I Work
Marie Cange

Discussion Preview

1. Discuss what kinds of jobs there are at an airport. Who works outside? Who works inside? List the jobs/people on the blackboard. Group the jobs into different categories.
2. Ask students how a parking lot works. Ask them to name different buildings or other places which need parking lots.

Picture Preview

1. Ask students to identify the person in the picture, what he is doing, and what his job is called. Students may identify the job as *toll collector* or *tollbooth attendant*, as well as *cashier*. Discuss other places where there are cashiers, such as stores and cafeterias. This can help clarify what a cashier does.

2. Ask students to name the small building where this man is working, to elicit the word *tollbooth*. Discuss what a toll is. Ask them to name places where there are tollbooths.

Comprehension

- **True or False**

  1. F   2. T   3. F   4. T   5. T   6. T   7. F

- **Fill-in**

  1. there   4. Usually
  2. But   5. always
  3. First

Language Skills

- **Vocabulary Review**

  airport, parking lot, terminal, tollbooth, cashier

- **Structure Practice: Prepositions**

  1. in   4. under
  2. at   5. from
  3. near   6. in

- **Structure Practice**

  Answers will vary. If you wish, students can ask each other questions with *How long* to elicit the answers to this exercise.

Follow-up

- **Let's Talk about It**

  1. in a parking lot, in a tollbooth, at the airport
  2. cashier
  3. Sometimes she drives, or goes by car. Sometimes she must take the subway and then a bus.
  4. 10
  5. At a parking lot, a cashier works in a tollbooth, collects money for parking when people leave; for other places, answers will vary.
  6. Answers will vary.

- **What's Your Story?**

  Alternative topic: Describe the airport in your town. (Refer to Let's Talk about It #6, or tell about an airport in the United States.)

13 New on the Job
Maria Velasquez

Discussion Preview

1. Ask students to describe different feelings people can have when they are new on a job. List these on the board. Group them as good or bad feelings.

2. Ask students to name places (post office, grocery store, doctor's office, etc.) where they have trouble understanding when someone speaks English to them. Ask them how they feel when this happens.

Picture Preview

Discuss students' ideas about the feelings of the women in the picture. Suggested questions: Do these women look happy or sad? Why do you think they look so serious? Do you think the work is interesting or boring? Do you think the women are friends with each other? Do they talk while they work, or help each other?

Comprehension

- **True or False**

    1. F   2. F   3. T   4. F   5. T   6. T

- **Fill-in**

    1. first   5. understand
    2. hard   6. nervous
    3. cousin   7. hotel
    4. child

Language Skills

- **Compound Words**

    nobody, something, downtown, everything

    other words: nothing, somebody, everybody

- **Structure Practice: Singular and Plural**

    1. countries   3. cities
    2. salaries   4. babies

- **Structure Practice: Verbs**
  1. work
  2. say
  3. works
  4. helps
  5. know
  6. knows
  7. needs

Follow-up

- **Let's Talk about It**
  1. in a belt factory
  2. because nobody knows her; also because nobody helps her, she can't speak English, she's nervous, she has to learn everything, and she can't understand what people say to her
  3. Maria's cousin
  4. because she can't speak to people, she doesn't know what people want her to do, and she doesn't understand what people say to her
  5. about one month
  6. maybe a hotel downtown
  7. cleaning lady

- **What's Your Story?**
  Alternative topics: Tell about a situation in which you were nervous. Tell about a situation in which you sometimes have trouble understanding English. (Refer to Discussion Preview #2.)

 14 The Boss and the Supervisor
Valentina Rivas

Discussion Preview

1. Ask working students about their supervisors. Students can also tell about a supervisor at a previous job. Suggested questions: Who is the supervisor? Where is he or she from? How old is the supervisor? What does this person do in his or her job? Does this person help the employees or make the job more difficult? How do you get along with your supervisor?
2. Discuss the differences between a supervisor and a boss. Companies may use these terms in different ways.

Picture Preview

Suggested questions: What is the man in the picture doing? What is he working with? Where do you think he is working? Why is the man wearing rubber gloves? Why is he wearing a cap (shower cap) to cover his hair? What do you think will happen to the pills after they leave this man?

Comprehension

- **True or False**
  1. T   2. F   3. F   4. T   5. T   6. F

- **Who's in the story?**

  1. boss
  2. employee
  3. boss
  4. supervisor
  5. supervisor
  6. boss
  7. supervisor
  8. employee

Language Skills

- **Structure Practice: Prepositions**

  1. in
  2. at
  3. of
  4. into
  5. with
  6. in
  7. in

- **Structure Practice: Verbs**

  1. work
  2. like
  3. packs
  4. makes
  5. looks
  6. comes
  7. sits, counts
  8. like

- **Structure Practice: Adjectives**

  1. *friendly boss*
  2. good work
  3. large book
  4. white face
  5. little room

Follow-up

- **Let's Talk about It**
  1. She works in a pill packing plant; she packs pills; she works on a line.

2. He is the line leader; he stands at the end of the line; he makes sure their work is good; he looks at the pill boxes.

3. friendly and helpful

4. He works with the money; he writes down the company's expenses; he writes down how much money the plant makes; he keeps the accounts; sometimes he comes into the packing room.

5. not much time

6. He never smiles; he is alone a lot. Other possible answers: He likes to be alone; he doesn't like the workers; he is unhappy; he is lonely; he likes math.

7. Answers will vary.

- **What's Your Story?**
  Alternative topic: Compare some aspect of your life (home, daily schedule, car, etc.) to that aspect of a friend's life.

15 Help from My Friends
Sergio Cabrera

Discussion Preview

Ask students to make two lists: jobs where knowing English matters a great deal and jobs where knowing English doesn't matter so much. Compare the lists and discuss.

Picture Preview

Ask students what they think is the relationship of the men in the picture. Suggested questions: What are some things friends do together? What are some things friends do for each other?

Comprehension

- **True or False**
  1. F   2. T   3. F   4. F   5. F   6. T

- **Fill-in**
  1. friends   4. application
  2. promotion   5. decorate
  3. employees   6. difficult

Language Skills

- **Word Families**

  1. apply
  2. promotion
  3. application
  4. promoted
  5. applied

- **Word Families**

  1. teacher (schoolteacher)
  2. painter (housepainter)
  3. worker
  4. writer
  5. singer
  6. driver
  7. reporter (news reporter)

- **Capital Letters: Names of Places**

  1. Chestnut Street
  2. Fenway Park
  3. Acme Trucking Company
  4. Fisher's Restaurant
  5. Golden Gate Bridge

Follow-up

- **Let's Talk about It**

  1. He was a pot washer; his first job is/was the one he has now.
  2. He helped/helps decorate party rooms.
  3. Ashbourne Country Club
  4. his friends
  5. for just two months
  6. because his friends knew about it and helped him, because the country club needed employees, because he didn't have to speak English to get the job

- **What's Your Story?**

  Alternative topics: Tell about how you started taking English lessons. Tell about how a friend got a job.

Book 2

The Working Experience **Lesson Notes**

 **My Work Dream**
Sergio Cabrera

Discussion Preview

1. Ask students to name methods of transportation (e.g., plane, truck, bus, train, taxi). Discuss the names of people professionally connected with each.
2. Ask students professions which require a training license or certificate. Examples: bus driver, beautician, nurse, car mechanic.

Picture Preview

1. Do you enjoy flying (as a passenger)? Have you ever flown a plane? Would you like to be a pilot? Do you think flying a plane would be a good job?
2. What training do you need to become a pilot? Do you think it is easy or difficult to learn to fly a plane?

Comprehension

- **True or False**
  1. F   2. T   3. T   4. F   5. F

- **Complete the Sentence**
  English, license, aviation, profession, pilot, flew, magazines, private, airport, training

Language Skills

- **Vocabulary Review**

  1. b   2. a   3. c   4. b   5. c

- **Word Families**

1. north	5. Southern
2. south	6. West
3. east	7. northern, South
4. western	

- **Structure Practice: Verbs**

1. *studying*	*studies*
2. applying	applies
3. crying	cries
4. carrying	carries
5. multiplying	multiplies
6. marrying	marries

- **Structure Practice: Prepositions**

  in, about, at, for, after

- **Capital Letters: Names of Languages**

1. Chinese	4. Korean
2. French	5. Italian
3. Russian	

- **Structure Practice**

  Answers will vary. You can also ask questions that will prompt students to expand on their responses.

Follow-up

- **A Closer Look**

  1. b   2. a   3. d

  Explain the underlined word: Sergio wants to leave his current job and become a pilot.

- **Let's Talk about Aviation**

  1. from magazines, from a pilot, from flying, from a training school
  2. go to a training school, learn to fly, get a license

3. at an airport

4. possible responses: travel to different places, see beautiful scenes, feel excitement from flying

5. possible responses: too much travel, too much time away from home, tiring work, danger of accidents

- **What's Your Story?**

  Alternative topics: How will you achieve your work/career goals? What training is required for your job, or for the job you hope to get?

2 A Working Mother
Maria Vegas

Discussion Preview

Suggested questions: Do mothers in your native country work outside the home? Is it common or unusual? What jobs can/do they get? Why do they work outside the home? Who helps them take care of their children?

Picture Preview

1. What is this woman doing? Where do you think she is working? In general, what is her work called?

2. What else do you think she will do as part of the housecleaning? Is her work hard or easy? Do you think she gets much money for her work?

Comprehension

- **True or False**

  1. T   2. F   3. F   4. F   5. F   6. F

- **Complete the Sentence**

  work, needed, cleaned, mornings, swept, scrubbed, washed, dusted, paid

Language Skills

- **Vocabulary Review**

  worked, cleaned, swept, washed, scrubbed, dusted

  This exercise and the following one also provide an opportunity to practice the pronunciation of past tense endings.

- **Structure Practice: Past Tense**
  1. worked
  2. wanted
  3. stayed
  4. cleaned
  5. washed
  6. needed

- **Structure Practice: Present and Past Tense**
  1. came
  2. pays
  3. need
  4. had
  5. went
  6. is (*was* may also be correct)
  7. swept
  8. stayed

- **Capital Letters: Beginning Sentences**
  1. *In*
  2. My
  3. Her
  4. They
  5. She

Follow-up

- **Let's Talk about It**
  1. Her husband was gone; she had four young children to take care of.
  2. Three children went to school, and her mother stayed with the baby.
  3. She worked for an old lady. She cleaned house, swept, scrubbed, dusted, and washed clothes.
  4. She was paid every two weeks with a check.
  5. Answers will vary. Possible responses: she hopes to find a better job or to make more money.
  6. Answers will vary.

- **What's Your Story?**
  Alternative topic: Compare women's jobs in your native country to women's jobs in the United States.

 3 **My Nursing Career**
Chrisanta Gordies

Discussion Preview

1. When you were a child, did you have a job? Did you help your parents with their work or with tasks at home?

2. You may wish to ask if any students have training, skills, or work experience that they cannot yet put to use because they still need to learn English.

Picture Preview

1. Ask students about the woman in the picture and what she is doing. Ask what her job is. Students may say either nurse or doctor. Ask where she is working: in what room, what department, what sort of building.
2. What kind of training do you think she has had? Do you think she likes her work? Why or why not? How do you think she feels about babies?

Comprehension

- **True or False**
  1. F   2. T   3. F   4. T   5. T   6. T   7. F

- **Complete the Sentence**
  oldest, baby-sit, children, high school, hospital, pediatric

Language Skills

- **Vocabulary: Opposite Meaning**
  1. oldest   3. started
  2. completed/finished   4. youngest

- **Structure Practice**
  I like children, so I decided to become a nurse.

  I have to study so I can learn English.

  My husband was born in New York, so I followed him back there.

  I am the oldest of seven children, so I used to baby-sit a lot.

  I don't speak English well, so I don't have a job.

- **Capital Letters: Two-Word Place Names**

  Puerto Rico   Fort Lauderdale

  New York   South America

  San Francisco   New Mexico

Follow-up

- **Let's Talk about It**
  1. because she liked children
  2. for 14 years

3. She followed her husband back to New York.

4. to learn English, so she can get a job again

- **What's Your Story?**
  Alternative topic: What jobs are suitable for a person who likes children?

 ## 4 The Place Where I Work
Nguyen Tran

Discussion Preview

1. Ask students what hospital they use. Where is it? How do they get there? What does it look like? If students have not been to a hospital in the United States, ask them to describe at least the outside of a hospital they have seen in this country.
2. Discuss the different "sections" (Nguyen's word) or departments in a hospital (e.g., emergency room, X-ray department, operating rooms).

Picture Preview

Ask students to describe the hospital building in the picture. Make sure they understand the term *Medical Center* and that it sometimes means the same as *hospital* and sometimes refers to a smaller institution. Discuss the terms *emergency* and *trauma.* Discuss what happens in an emergency room.

Comprehension

- **True or False**
  1. T   2. F   3. F   4. T   5. F   6. T

- **Multiple Choice**
  1. a, b, c (Check that students understand "far from downtown.")
  2. b, c, d
  3. b, d
  4. a, b, d
  5. b, c
  6. a, b, d

Language Skills

- **Vocabulary Review**

  building, parking lot, entrance, elevator, section

  Practice: Answers will vary.

- **Structure Practice: Singular and Plural**

  1. bosses
  2. losses
  3. waitresses
  4. campuses
  5. classes
  6. dresses
  7. guesses

- **Structure Practice: Prepositions**

  1. in
  2. far from
  3. in front of
  4. behind
  5. inside
  6. on

- **Number Work**

  1. $3\frac{1}{2}$
  2. $\frac{1}{2}$
  3. $7\frac{1}{2}$
  4. $\frac{1}{2}$
  5. $10\frac{1}{2}$

Follow-up

- **Let's Talk about It**

  1. in a hospital
  2. She takes three buses and one train.
  3. one and a half hours
  4. three parking lots
  5. on one side of the building
  6. four: one for emergencies, two for visitors, one for employees
  7. She must have an ID card. Answers will vary.
  8. many elevators, special elevators for emergencies, different sections on each floor, sections for operations and X-rays, for example

- **What's Your Story?**

  Alternative topics: Tell about the hospital in your town or region in the United States or in your native country. (Refer to Discussion Preview #1.) Tell about a time you visited or were in a hospital.

5 Nervous at Work
Yvonne Largaespada

Discussion Preview

1. What was your first job (in any country)? How did you feel when you first started? Did you know any people at your job? How did they treat you? Did you know the language? How did you stop feeling nervous?

2. What are some situations that make you feel nervous?

Picture Preview

Discuss with students what they think the woman in the picture feels like, what the expression on her face suggests. Ask for their opinions of why she looks that way. Discuss situations that might make her look/feel that way.

Comprehension

- **True or False**
  1. T   2. F   3. T   4. T   5. F   6. T

- **Complete the Sentence**
  buttons, nervous, staring, self-conscious, loudspeaker, announcing, wrong

Language Skills

- **Vocabulary Review**
  1. staring   3. announcing
  2. loudspeaker   4. housewife

- **Compound Words**
  house—wife
  every—body
  any—more
  loud—speaker

- **Word Families**
  1. announcement 3. announcer
  2. announcing   4. announced

- **Structure Practice: Verbs**
  1. put
  2. stare
  3. announce
  4. tell
  5. work
  6. stay

Follow-up

- **Let's Talk about It**
  1. She put buttons on shirts.
  2. She thought everybody was staring at her; she didn't know English; she couldn't understand the announcements over the loudspeaker.
  3. She thought they were announcing her name and telling everybody she was doing her job wrong.
  4. She likes her job now; she isn't nervous anymore; she can do her work; she feels at home at her job.
  5. She says work is a way for her to forget her problems.

- **Thinking about the Story**

  In small groups, students can list pros and cons, and then discuss which is better.

- **What's Your Story?**

  Alternative topics: Tell about a situation in which you were nervous. (Refer to Discussion Preview #1.) Use ideas from the discussion for Thinking about the Story and develop an LEA about whether it is better to work or stay at home.

 6 **Benefits at Work**
Sergio Cabrera

Discussion Preview

1. Discuss what happens in a country when the economy is bad, in terms of jobs, salaries, prices, and so on. Ask students to identify a time in their country when the economy was bad. What happened?
2. Ask students to give examples of job benefits, ones they get and ones they know about but don't get. List these on the board and discuss which are the most important or valuable and which are the least important.

Picture Preview

What kinds of jobs are done at a gas station? Ask students if they think being a gas station attendant is a good job, in their native country and/or in the United States. If so, why? What is good about it? If not, why not? What are the problems?

Comprehension

- **True or False**
  1. F 2. T (before 1982) 3. F 4. F 5. F 6. T

Language Skills

- **Structure Practice: The Verb "To Be"**

  1. was   5. is
  2. am   6. are
  3. was   7. am
  4. were

- **Structure Practice: Past Tense**
  worked, had, wanted, changed, got, paid

- **Word Families**

  1. government   4. medicine
  2. medical   5. economy
  3. economic   6. governor

- **Number Work**
  $60, $800, $25, $350, $15, $620

- **Capital Letters**

  1. *Argentina*   3. United States
  2. Cambodia, Vietnam   4. Canada

Follow-up

- **Let's Talk about It**
  1. at a gas station
  2. about $60 per month
  3. In his opinion, it was a lot of money at that time.
  4. only some medical benefits if he got hurt

5. Sergio paid his own doctor bills.

6. Answers may vary; probably better, because he makes more money and has better benefits.

- **What's Your Story?**
  Alternative topic: Do people in your native country generally have health insurance or medical benefits? Who provides them?

7 Finding a Job
Mary Luz Soto

Discussion Preview

1. Discuss and have students list qualifications that are important when a person is looking for a job. Possible responses: past experience, training or education, personal characteristics such as strength or willingness to learn, skills such as typing or shorthand, etc. Ask students for their opinion of what qualifications are the most important.

2. Discuss and have students list problems that can hurt a person in his or her job search. The story mentions "no experience." Other possible responses: age, being a woman, prejudice, the slow job market, limited English skills, etc.

Picture Preview

What is the woman in the picture doing? How could her ability to sew (and perhaps also design) clothes help her get a job? What jobs could she do with this skill?

Comprehension

- **True or False**
  1. F   2. F   3. F   4. T   5. T   6. F

- **Time Sequence**
  3, 6, 4, 2, *1*, 5

Language Skills

- **Vocabulary Review**
  Find at least seven of the eight additional words: *work,* hire, experience, interview, employers, employee, company, manager, job

- **Structure Practice: Past Tense**

  came, was, had, went, made, told, gave, felt

- **Compound Words**

  nothing, nobody, nowhere, myself, something

  two more words: somewhere, somebody

- **Structure Practice: Pronouns**

  1. me
  2. me
  3. they
  4. them
  5. He
  6. him
  7. he, me
  8. I

- **Number Work**

  1. nineteen—19
  2. fifteen—15
  3. ninety—90
  4. thirteen—13
  5. thirty-one—31
  6. eighteen—18

Follow-up

- **A Closer Look**

  1. c   2. c   3. c   4. b

- **Let's Talk about It**

  1. in an apartment, in Philadelphia

  2. because she didn't have any experience at any job

  3. because he liked her clothes and saw that she could sew very well

  4. Answers will vary. Possible responses: because she had to learn new job responsibilities, because she wanted to do a good job.

- **What's Your Story?**

  Alternative topic: Tell about your first days or weeks in the United States. What good things happened? What difficulties did you face?

 My Bosses
Sergio Cabrera

Discussion Preview

1. Ask students to think of as many ways as they can to complete the sentence "A good boss...." Bring students together to share their responses and discuss.

2. Similarly, ask students to complete the sentence "A bad boss..." and then discuss.

Picture Preview

Ask students if their boss explains things to them and shows them how to do their job, the way one woman in the picture is doing for the other. Ask how they feel about this.

Comprehension

- **True or False**
  1. T   2. T   3. F   4. F   5. F

- **Multiple Choice**
  1. a, b, c
  2. a, b
  3. b, c, d

Language Skills

- **Vocabulary Review**
  1. decorate   4. check
  2. mistake   5. opinion
  3. inspect

- **Structure Practice: Past Tense**
  1. made   5. taught
  2. gave   6. came
  3. knew   7. had
  4. told

- **Word Families**
  1. Vietnam   4. Korea
  2. America   5. China
  3. Argentina   6. Ethiopia

- **Structure Practice: Singular and Plural**
  1. bosses   5. glasses
  2. countries   6. businesses
  3. parties   7. canvases
  4. cities   8. babies

- **Structure Practice: Pronouns**

  1. My
  2. me
  3. his
  4. him
  5. him
  6. He
  7. me
  8. He

Follow-up

- **A Closer Look**

  1. *b*   2. a   3. b   4. c   5. c   6. a   7. a

- **Let's Talk about Sergio's Bosses**

  1. because he helped his boss a lot

  2. everything about the kitchen in the country club

  3. He inspected Sergio's work, told Sergio what was good and not good, gave Sergio ideas, taught Sergio how to fix his mistakes, inspected Sergio's work, and told Sergio when he had done a nice job.

  4. He never checked Sergio's work, never checked on problems or mistakes, and never gave his opinion of Sergio's work.

  5. everything about decorating rooms for parties

- **What's Your Story?**

  Alternative topic: Tell about a teacher you have had who was helpful. Tell about a good boss that you have worked for. Tell about a bad boss. Have you ever been a boss? Do you think you were a good boss?

 **Getting Ahead**
Haydee Quintana

Discussion Preview

What does it mean to get ahead? What are some ways to get ahead, in your job or in any job? Are these ways the same or different in your native country and in the United States?

Picture Preview

Use the picture to elicit some of the key terms in the story. Ask students to describe or guess what the people in the picture are doing. Possible responses: typing, preparing bills or some other mailing, or sorting papers. Ask them which department in a company this might be. Discuss other jobs that are done in a clerical department.

Comprehension

- **True or False**
  1. T   2. F   3. F   4. T   5. T   6. T
- **Multiple Choice**
  1. a, b, c, d   3. a, b, c
  2. b, c   4. a, b, d

Language Skills

- **Vocabulary Review**
  People: bosses, workers, managers, owner, assistant personnel director
  Activities: packing, pressing, shipping, trimming, filing
- **Structure Practice**
  Answers will vary. If you wish, students can work in pairs to complete these sentences.
- **Structure Practice: Verbs**
  shipping, learning, packing, putting, doing, filing, growing, hiring

Follow-up

- **A Closer Look**
  1. c   2. b   3. d   4. a (possibly also d)   5. c
  Explain the underlined word: I like to keep busy.
- **Let's Talk about It**
  1. the clerical department
  2. a computer/computers
  3. how different departments work; also, Spanish and English
  4. She likes to work, and she likes to keep busy.
  5. She says she likes to work and does a good job; she also says she is friendly and always helps others. Students may have other ideas.
- **Thinking about the Story**
  Ask students to identify Haydee's ideas about how to get ahead. Then ask them for their own suggestions. (Refer to Discussion Preview.) List student responses on the board. Discuss which ways they feel are the most important ones.

- **What's Your Story?**
  Alternative topic: What are some uses for computers, at work or in other situations? What jobs or work situations might require knowing two languages?

10 A Problem at Work
Kenny Pak

Discussion Preview

1. Ask students to identify places where they have the biggest problems because English is their new language. Possible responses: post office, supermarket, doctor's office, etc. Ask about the kinds of language problems they have had.

2. Ask students to list three jobs for which they think English is very important and three jobs for which they think English is not so important. Have them work in pairs or small groups. Then bring them together to discuss their lists. Ask them to give reasons why English is or is not important in those jobs.

Picture Preview

Where is the man in the picture working? What do you think he is doing? What else might be part of his job? What are some of the food items he probably sells? What kinds of job problems do you think he might have?

Comprehension

- **True or False**
  1. F   2. F   3. F   4. T   5. F

Language Skills

- **Vocabulary Review**
  1. b   2. d   3. b   4. c

- **Structure Practice: Past Tense**
  had, knew, said, made, went, taught

- **Two-Word Phrases**

bus stop	living room
bus station	fire station
ice cream	train station
fire escape	

- **Punctuation**
  1. They say, "I want a hot dog."
  2. "Do you speak English?" he asked.
  3. "No," I answered. "Just a little bit."
  4. "Oh my," he said. "That's no good."
  5. The teacher asked, "Do you understand this lesson?"
  6. "Yes," the students answered. "We understand everything."
  7. "Very good," the teacher said.

Follow-up

- **A Closer Look**

  Students should identify any 8 of these 10 words.

hamburgers	hot dog
cheeseburgers	cooked
salads	ham
sandwiches	grill
eat	customers

- **Let's Talk about Kenny's Job**
  1. He didn't know the language of the job; he made a lot of mistakes; his customers weren't polite; his English wasn't good enough; he cooked things wrong for customers.
  2. They told him what they wanted to eat; they asked him for hamburgers, hot dogs, and other food items.
  3. because Kenny cooked something wrong and didn't speak English well
  4. because he speaks better English, he can understand the guests when they talk to him, he knows the vocabulary of the snack bar, he cooks good food, and he makes great hamburgers

- **What's Your Story?**

  Alternative topics: Tell about a problem you have or had at work (not caused by language difficulties). What special vocabulary did you learn for your job? Did you have any problems because of language when you first came to the United States? Tell about them.

11 My Own Business
Maria Elizabeth Torres

Discussion Preview

1. What does it mean to run your own business? What sorts of businesses do individuals own or run?
2. What are some of the problems or disadvantages of having your own business? What are some positive features or advantages?

Picture Preview

What is the woman in the picture doing? Where is she working? Who do you think the two boys are? What are they probably doing? What might be the advantages and disadvantages of working at home?

Comprehension

- **True or False**

  1. F   2. T   3. F   4. T   5. T   6. F   7. T
- **Time Sequence**

  5, 4, 2, 6, 3, 1

Language Skills

- **Word Families**

1. unload	3. load
2. loaded	4. unloaded

  The word *employ*

1. employee	4. employed
2. unemployed	5. employer (*employee* is also possible)
3. unemployment	6. employment

- **Structure Practice**
  1. There was no war then, but the army was always training soldiers.
  2. With my own business, I don't have benefits, but I'm still doing well.

Follow-up

- **Let's Talk about It**
  1. in her home
  2. her mother
  3. She sewed in factories.
  4. Maria says she's still doing well. She probably also doesn't mind because she likes her job.

- **Thinking about the Story**
  Students can work in pairs or small groups and list things that make businesses work and businesses fail. One student from each group can record the reasons, and another can report the results.

- **What's Your Story?**
  Alternative topics: What are the problems and/or benefits of having your own business? (Refer to Discussion Preview #2.) What are the advantages and/or disadvantages of working in your own home? (Refer to Picture Preview.) Tell about a business you would like to start.

 **12 Our Family Store**
Maria Velasquez

Discussion Preview

What occupations did your parents have? Where did they work? In which country or countries? In what cities or areas did they work? In what company or business? List and compare the responses.

Picture Preview

1. Ask students to describe what they see in the picture of a small grocery store. Help them with any vocabulary words they cannot supply.
2. Ask students if they now shop, or have ever shopped, in a grocery store like this one. Ask them to describe it.

Comprehension

- **True or False**
  1. F   2. T   3. F   4. T   5. F

Language Skills

- **Word Families**
  1. redo   3. remodeled
  2. refile   4. renamed

- **Compound Words**

  upstairs   afternoon

  downstairs   supermarket

- **Capital Letters: Days of the Week**

  1. Friday and Saturday

  Answers for 2.–6. will vary.

- **Structure Practice: Adjectives**
  1. *My father had a little supermarket.*
  2. The store was small.
  3. It was red and white.
  4. When he was young, my father worked hard.
  5. Now my father is old.

- **Number Work**

2 second	9 ninth
4 fourth	7 seventh
5 fifth	3 third
8 eighth	*1* first
10 tenth	6 sixth

- **Structure Practice: Past Tense**

  was, lived, had, sold, loved, came, grew, worked, gave, stayed

Follow-up

- **A Closer Look**
  1. c, d   4. a, b, d
  2. b, c, d   5. b
  3. b, c

- **Let's Talk about the Family Store**
  1. The front was red and white; the store was very pretty; it had two floors. Students may have other ideas as well.
  2. The family's home was upstairs, and the store was downstairs.
  3. food and beer, but no clothes
  4. Maria's father, Maria and her little brothers, members of the family, one employee, a man. Answers will vary.
  5. every Friday and Saturday
  6. Answers will vary.

- **What's Your Story?**
  Alternative topics: How do your children help you around the house? Tell about your parents, their lives and/or their work.

13 Day Off
Maria Velasquez

Discussion Preview

1. Ask students when stores and businesses are closed in their native countries. What hours during the day? Which days of the week? What times of the year? Ask why they are closed at those times.
2. Ask students what activities they (or people) like to do on their days off.

Picture Preview

Ask students to describe the people in the picture. What do you think they are doing? What do you think their relationship is? Why do you think they are sitting together like this? How do you think they feel about being together? Do they look pleased or not?

Comprehension

- **True or False**
  1. F   2. T   3. F   4. F   5. T   6. F

- **Time Sequence**
  4, 3, 6, 1, 5, 2

Language Skills

- **Word Families**
  1. fresher
  2. taller
  3. stronger
  4. colder
  5. faster
  6. newer

- **Structure Practice: Comparative Adjectives**
  1. *newer, socks*
  2. fresher, milk
  3. taller, Robin
  4. faster, Andy
  5. colder, Vietnam
  6. stronger, Kenny

- **Structure Practice: Prepositions**
  in, in, at, for, to, on, with, after

- **Number Work**
  1. 11:00
  2. 7:00
  3. 10:30
  4. 10:00
  5. 11:30
  6. 6:45

Follow-up

- **A Closer Look**
  1. c   2. a   3. b   4. c

- **Let's Talk about It**
  1. Yes, she has brothers.
  2. She worked in the store for two or three hours in the morning. Then they all got ready for church and had something to eat together.
  3. sat by the river, laughed and joked
  4. a pretty dress
  5. Probably she liked it because she didn't work long hours, she spent time with her family, they laughed and joked, and they relaxed.

- **What's Your Story?**
  Alternative topic: When you were growing up, what were some favorite family activities on days off?

14 My Job Expectations
Shiao Chu Sun

Discussion Preview

1. When you came to the United States, did you know exactly what would happen to you? Did you have any ideas or guesses? What were your expectations about your future life in the United States?

2. What is experience? How is experience useful in a job? Did you have any work experience when you got your current job?

Picture Preview

Where do you think these two men are working? What are they looking at? What do you think they might be talking about?

Comprehension

- **True or False**
  1. T   2. T   3. F   4. F   5. T   6. T   7. F

- **Complete the Sentence**
  experience, textile business, quality control, employed, manufactured, exported

Language Skills

- **Vocabulary Review**
  cotton, nylon, silk
  other possibilities: wool, velvet, denim, polyester, rayon

- **Number Work**
  100—one hundred
  1,000—one thousand
  10,000—ten thousand
  100,000—one hundred thousand
  1,000,000—one million
  Write the number words:
  two million
  one hundred
  four thousand
  thirty thousand

Underline and write number words:

1. *two hundred thousand dollars—$200,000*
2. three hundred—300
3. five thousand—5,000
4. ten thousand—10,000
5. a million dollars—$1,000,000

Follow-up

- **Let's Talk about It**
  1. quality control
  2. Shanghai
  3. cotton, nylon, silk, and other fabrics
  4. sewing pieces of fabric together to make clothes
  5. Possible answers: The factory where she works is smaller; she sews, rather than working in quality control; the factory makes clothes, not fabric; she has to do many things she hasn't done before.
  6. Answers will vary. Students should give reasons for their responses.

- **Thinking about the Story**
  In pairs, small groups, or in a larger group, students can list and discuss what happened when they or people they know came to America and looked for a job.

- **What's Your Story?**
  Alternative topic: How can work experience help you get a new job?

15 Getting Used to My Job
Mattie Lane

Discussion Preview

Suggested questions: How do people sometimes feel in new situations? When you first started your job, how did you feel? What were the other workers like? How did your supervisor treat you? If you felt nervous or uncomfortable at first, when did you begin to feel good? What made your feelings change?

Picture Preview

1. What is the woman in the picture doing? What equipment is she using? Where do you think she is? Is it common to find a microwave oven in a workplace? What about a coffee pot, like the one next to the microwave oven?

2. What are the physical conditions at the place where you work? Is there a cafeteria, or lunchroom? What can you eat/buy/make there? Is there a refrigerator, stove, microwave oven, etc.?

Comprehension

- **True or False**

  1. F   2. T   3. T   4. F   5. T   6. T

- **Complete the Sentence**

  feel sick, hide, angry, other workers, friendly, supervisor, got along

Language Skills

- **Vocabulary: Similar Meanings**

  1. sick   4. polite

  2. workers   5. installed

  3. angry   6. bathrooms

- **Compound Words**

  with—out

  any—more

  bath—room

  work—place

- **Two-Word Phrases**

  air conditioning   microwave ovens

  bathroom facilities   cafeteria area

Follow-up

- **Let's Talk about It**

  1. She thought the other employees would hide her work; she didn't like working; she was nervous.

  2. They seemed friendly; they became like another family.

  3. keep the business going and avoid laying off workers

4. installed air conditioning, improved the bathrooms and the cafeteria area, put microwave ovens in the cafeteria

5. Answers will vary.

- **Thinking about the Story**

  Students can list in pairs or small groups what makes an employer good or bad. Then they can share and discuss their responses.

- **What's Your Story?**

  Alternative topics: Describe your workplace. Use ideas from the Thinking about the Story discussion and develop an LEA about what makes an employer good or bad.

Book 3

The Working Experience **Lesson Notes**

1 Getting Paid
Yvonne Largaespada

Discussion Preview/Picture Preview

How did you feel when you got your first paycheck? How do you feel now when you get paid? Do you get paid by check or in cash?

Comprehension

- **True or False**
  1. T   2. T   3. F   4. F   5. F   6. F

- **Complete the Sentence**

  nervous, how much, because, depended on, my mother, either, give her something

Language Skills

- **Vocabulary Expansion**
  1. sick time
  2. social security
  3. bereavement
  4. workman's compensation
  5. overtime
  6. unemployment
  7. disability
  8. health insurance
  9. vacation pay

- **Punctuation: Quotation Marks**
  1. Yvonne says, "I want to become old working in this factory."
  2. no quotation marks

3. Yvonne kept thinking, "What am I going to get paid?"

4. no quotation marks

Follow-up

- **A Closer Look**

Answers will vary. Students' responses can then be the basis for further discussion.

- **A Closer Look: Inference**

Explain that these inference questions do not necessarily have right or wrong answers. Students may give different answers based on what the story says and how their own experiences and ideas enter into their judgments. Students should give the information from the story they have to support their answers.

- **Let's Talk about It**

1. Yvonne was very nervous, because she didn't know how much she would get. She was also happy, because the money was hers, and she didn't have to depend on her mother for help.

2. No, she doesn't send money to her family, because her husband doesn't want her to. He says they need all the money they earn.

3. because she gets paid, the benefits are good, and the union is good

- **What's Your Story?**

Alternative topic: Should children help their parents or families, financially or in other ways? Why or why not?

Job Hunting
Vincent Lei

Discussion Preview

Discuss different ways to find a job. Ask students to name different methods of job hunting which are customary in their native countries.

Picture Preview

Discuss want ads and whether they are an effective way to find a job. Discuss the information that might appear in a want ad. Ask students if they ever responded to a want ad and what response they got in return.

Comprehension

- **True or False**

  1. F   2. F   3. F   4. T   5. T   6. F

- **Multiple Choice**

  1. b   2. b   3. c   4. c

- **Word Families**

  1. govern   5. arrange
  2. appoint   6. employ
  3. advertise   7. commit
  4. manage

- **Structure Practice: Time Signals**

  After, When, During, First, Then, Now

- **Initials**

  1. g   4. a   7. c
  2. e   5. h   8. f
  3. i   6. b   9. d

- **Vocabulary Review**

  job hunt, ads, qualifications, interview, appointment, resume

Follow-up

- **A Closer Look**

  1. possible answers: type of position, name and address of company, name of contact person, required qualifications, hours, salary

  2. possible answers: name, address, telephone number, education, work experience, career goals, references

  3. possible answers: finding out about the company, dressing neatly, thinking of questions to ask the interviewer, thinking of questions the interviewer might ask you, finding out where the company is located, leaving early to get to the appointment on time

- **Let's Talk about It**

  1. possible responses: because he didn't have to write a resume, because the government arranged interviews, because he didn't have to take a job he didn't want

  2. possible responses: because he needs to know how to use want ads and to write resumes and letters of application, because English is not his native language, because job hunting is very different in this country

3. possible responses: because he had a college education, because the government would help him find another job, because many companies and factories would give him an interview

4. possible responses: the language difference, the different ways of job hunting in America, the fact that the government doesn't help with the job hunt

- **What's Your Story?**
  Alternative topic: Tell about different ways of finding a job in this country. Which one do you think is best? (Refer to Discussion Preview.)

3 Where I Work
Tan Trinh

Discussion Preview/Picture Preview

Ask students to describe the places where they work. Ask if there are special offices, departments, or different areas of activity. Students who don't work can describe their school or another building.

Comprehension

- **True or False**
  1. F   2. T   3. F   4. F   5. F   6. F

- **Complete the Sentence**
  building, entrance, ID card, business computer, swimming pool, restaurant, game

Language Skills

- **Vocabulary Review**
  Answers will vary, based on individual experiences.

- **Structure Practice: Verbs**
  1. living   4. dancing
  2. shining   5. gambling
  3. driving
  Use the verbs:
  1. driving   3. shining
  2. gambling, dancing   4. Living

- **Punctuation**
  1. This class has people from Ethiopia, Vietnam, and Puerto Rico.
  2. I always bring a notebook, a pen, and paper to class.
  3. Students, teachers, and parents came to the meeting.
  4. This house has one living room, two bedrooms, a kitchen, and a bathroom.
  5. My mother, father, sister, and brother will live there.

- **Capitals: Cities**
  1. Mexico City   4. Los Angeles
  2. Cape Town   5. San Salvador
  3. Hong Kong

  two more cities: Possible responses include New York, Addis Ababa, Phnom Penh, Tel Aviv, New Delhi, and Rio de Janeiro.

Follow-up

- **A Closer Look**
  1. c   2. d   3. b   4. a

- **Let's Talk about It**
  1. casinos, tall buildings
  2. because so many people come to visit, to gamble, or to work there
  3. because parking lots next to the casinos would get too full if everyone parked in them
  4. They can swim, eat in the banquet rooms and the restaurants, go to night clubs, and gamble in the game rooms.
  5. because the casino does not want strange people walking around the business areas, perhaps because the owners are afraid someone might find a way to rob the casino
  6. because the casinos are exciting, attractive places, and because they like to gamble

- **What's Your Story?**
  Alternative topic: How do you get to work? How do you get to school?

4 Getting My First Job
Juan Vegas

Discussion Preview

Suggested questions: How did you find out about your first job? What information did your employer ask for? Did you have any experience in that work?

Picture Preview

What is the man in the picture doing? What do you think he is saying? What will he probably do next?

Comprehension

- **True or False**

  1. F   2. F   3. T   4. T   5. F   6. F

- **Time Sequence**

  3, 5, 2, 6, *1*, 4

Language Skills

- **Vocabulary Review**

  1. social security number   4. office

  2. sign   5. owner

  3. customers   6. experience

- **Capitalization and Punctuation**

  I was riding on the bus with my friend **Edward**. **It** was going north on **Vermont Avenue**. **Edward** saw a **Help Wanted** sign in front of a place called **Smith's Car Wash**. **We** decided to stop and ask about the job.

  All I remember about the owner of the car wash was that he asked me for my social security number and my age. **I** gave him the number and told him **I** was 27 years old.

- **Structure Practice: Past and Past Continuous Tense**

  1. were riding   4. was living

  2. was talking   5. worked

  3. talked

Follow-up

- **Let's Talk about It**
  1. His friend Edward saw a Help Wanted sign.
  2. because Juan knew little English and Edward's English was better
  3. his age and social security number, and his experience
  4. Answers will vary.
  5. Answers will vary.

- **Thinking about the Story**

  Answers can vary greatly. Possible responses: because they have experience, because they don't have experience and will work for low wages, because they know English, because they don't know English and will work for low wages, because they are good workers.

- **What's Your Story?**

  Alternative topic: What are some jobs that do not require previous experience?

5 Nursery School Teacher
Augustin Ortiz

Discussion Preview

Suggested questions: What training is required in order to teach in a nursery school? What training is desirable?

Picture Preview

What activities are going on in the picture? What do teachers in a nursery school do with their pupils?

Comprehension

- **True or False**
  1. T   2. T   3. F   4. F   5. T   6. F

- **Multiple Choice**
  1. c   2. a   3. d   4. b

Language Skills

- **Vocabulary**

1. social work	4. exercise
2. area	5. counseling
3. children	6. earned

- **Structure Practice**

  Answers will vary, based on individual experiences.

- **Vocabulary: Abbreviations**

  B.A.—Bachelor of Arts

  B.S.—Bachelor of Science

  A.A.—Associate of Arts or Associate's Degree

  M.S.—Master of Science

  G.E.D.—General Equivalency Diploma or high school equivalency diploma

  M.D.—Medical Doctor

  Ph.D.—A doctoral degree

Follow-up

- **Let's Talk about It**

  1. preschool age, between three and five years old

  2. poor, low income, no work, no education, not enough money

  3. so the children could have exercise to help them develop their muscles

  4. by providing counseling to help them deal with family problems

  5. Answers will vary.

  6. He had a B.A. in elementary education. He also did social work.

- **Thinking about the Story**

  When students work on this activity, they can divide into two groups, each representing one of the possible answers to the question. Each group can list its reasons and report them to the larger group. For each group, one student can record the reasons and another can report to the larger group.

- **What's Your Story?**

  Alternative topics: Tell about the schools in your native country. Tell about your first teacher. Develop an LEA based on the Thinking about the Story discussion.

6 Out of Work
Ruben Amaro

Discussion Preview

Discuss general reasons why people lose their jobs. Possible responses: a company closing down, getting fired for not doing a good job, getting laid off because of cutbacks in personnel, a machine taking over a job, or a company leaving the area.

Picture Preview

What happens when a factory closes down? What happens to the people who worked there?

Comprehension

- **True or False**
  1. F   2. F   3. T   4. T

- **Complete the Sentence**
  closed down, products, sales job, similar job, problem, 40, an old man

Language Skills

- **Structure Practice: Auxiliary Verbs**
  couldn't, wouldn't, didn't, can't, won't, don't

- **Word Families**

  1. write   5. happen
  2. lose   6. work
  3. tell   7. have
  4. decide   8. get

- **Vocabulary Review**
  mentions, inflation, similar, overseas, gamble

Follow-up

- **A Closer Look**
  1. b   2. c   3. d   4. b   5. c

- **Let's Talk about It**
  1. The company had to close down because it couldn't pay for products from overseas.

2. He says that companies in Mexico don't like to hire people who had similar jobs with other companies, and that he was over 40 years old.

3. Answers will vary.

4. Answers will vary.

5. Students might suggest that it would be a good idea for Ruben to stay in Mexico because he knows more people in the job market there, because he has more connections, and because he knows the language.

   Alternatively, students might think it would be a good idea for Ruben to come to America because his job opportunities are wider, he would not have problems because of his age and experience, and he has friends to help him find a job.

- **What's Your Story?**

  Alternative topic: What are some reasons why people lose their jobs? (Refer to Discussion Preview.)

7 A Busy Time
Maria Velasquez

Discussion Preview

Ask students to tell about a time of the day or week when they are very busy. They can also describe a busy time at a store they go to, or at a bank or post office.

Picture Preview

What are the men in the picture doing? Describe the store in the picture. Do you ever shop at a grocery store like this one? Tell about that store.

Comprehension

True or False
1. F   2. T   3. T   4. F   5. F   6. F

Language Skills

- **Vocabulary Review**

  five foods: rice, chicken or hen, fish, tomato sauce, salt

  four things to drink: beer, whiskey, Coke, orange juice

  four ways to pay: cash, checks, welfare food coupons, credit

- **Structure Practice: Singular and Plural Verbs**

  1. men
  2. checks
  3. rice
  4. Saturdays
  5. customers
  6. salt
  7. days
  8. people
  9. coupons
  10. fish

- **Structure Practice: Past Tense**

  got up, came, bought, made, lost, paid, got, told

- **Punctuation**

  "Do you want rice?" we asked. "Do you want a chicken, a hen?"

  "Oh yes," they said. "Yes, yes."

  Sometimes people got angry because they were in a hurry. "I want it fast!" they said. "I have to do this, I have to do that!"

  People paid with cash, with checks, and with welfare food coupons. People paid on credit, too.

- **Structure Practice**

  Answers will vary, based on students' experiences.

Follow-up

- **A Closer Look**

  1. b   2. b   3. a   4. a

- **Let's Talk about It**

  1. to get everything ready at the store, because these were busy days in the store and there was a lot of work to do
  2. so the salespeople could check what to get for them and could work faster
  3. because it slowed down the salespeople, who had to remember everything the customers wanted or ask them what they wanted
  4. They stopped in quickly and asked for just one item, so the salespeople lost time selling just one item on a busy day.
  5. People got angry; people didn't want to wait.

- **What's Your Story?**

  Alternative topics: Tell about a time of the day or week when you are particularly busy. (Refer to Discussion Preview.) Describe the grocery store where you shop. (Refer to Picture Preview.)

8 Learning on the Job
Nelly Mariotta

Discussion Preview

How do people learn jobs? Who can help them learn? What kinds of jobs, or parts of a job, can people learn on their own?

Picture Preview

What do you think the people in the picture are talking about? What could their relationship be?

Comprehension

- **True or False**
  1. F   2. F   3. F   4. F   5. T   6. F   7. T

- **Time Sequence**
  2, 3, 4, 1, 5

- **Locating Information**
  Responses should include the information below.
  1. learning by watching other people, teaching oneself, asking questions, getting to know people, getting help from a supervisor
  2. operate the copy machine, answer the telephone, help people sign in and out, take checks, make receipts, register children for a summer program, keep an attendance list, give the children lunch and a snack
  3. cleaned, answered the phone, took messages

Language Skills

- **Word Families**
  1. operation   5. Registration
  2. register   6. attendance
  3. operate   7. attend, registration
  4. assistance

- **Structure Practice: Past Tense**
  came, knew, took, got, taught, took, paid, knew

- **Structure Practice**
  Answers will vary, based on students' experiences.

Follow-up

- **A Closer Look**

  1. a   2. c   3. a   4. a   5. c

- **Let's Talk about It**

  1. Possible responses: She watched other people, taught herself some things, got training from her supervisor, asked questions, and got to know people.

  2. She says her volunteer work became a paid job because she was always at work on time and never took a sick day.

  3. Possible responses: She likes learning new things; she likes working with people.

  4. because they knew she was a good worker

  5. Answers will vary.

- **What's Your Story?**

  Alternative topics: What do you enjoy about your job? Have you ever participated in activities at a community center? Tell about your experience.

Getting Ahead
Martha Manjulowicz

Discussion Preview

What kind of training do you need to work in a hospital? in a laboratory? What kinds of jobs are available in a research or medical laboratory?

Picture Preview

What is the woman in the picture doing? Where do you think she is working? What might her job be?

Comprehension

- **True or False**
  1. F   2. F   3. T   4. F   5. F   6. T

- **Complete the Sentence**

  piecework, machines, union, volunteer, civil service test, trainee, City Hall, technician

Language Skills

- **Structure Practice: Past Tense**

  came, got, left, became

  went, took, was, told, were

- **Vocabulary: Opposite Meanings**

  1. *paid*   4. volunteer

  2. hated   5. loved

  3. failed   6. passed

- **Structure Practice: Compound Sentences**

  1. I left the factory and worked as a volunteer in a city hospital.

  2. The doctor told me to go to City Hall and take the civil service test.

  3. I passed the test and became a paid trainee in the lab.

  4. Six months later, I took another test and became a histology technician.

Follow-up

- **Let's Talk about It**

  1. She probably didn't like it; it was hot, and it gave her bad dreams.

  2. to learn a new job

  3. the doctor in the laboratory

  4. She took tests which allowed her to become a paid trainee and then a technician; later, she took university courses to became a registered histology technician.

  5. by volunteering, by training on the job, by taking university courses

  6. They have to be trained in a university program.

- **Thinking about the Story**

  This exercise can be done with the whole group or in small groups. Students can say why they think it was easy or hard for Martha to get a job when she first came to the United States. When done in a group, the instructor or a student can list individual reasons on the board in columns marked *easy* and *hard*. Small groups can list their answers and reasons and report their findings back to the larger group. When the discussions are complete, students can think again about the question and, based on all the responses, reconsider their original responses.

- **What's Your Story?**
  Alternative topics: Did you ever dream about your work (or about school)? Tell about your dream. Tell about someone you know who has gotten ahead in his or her job.

10 Working
Georgette Lucce

Discussion Preview

Do people often leave their countries after a war? What are some reasons for doing this?

Picture Preview

What are the women in the picture making or working with? When do you think this picture was taken? Is it common or unusual for women to work with munitions in your country?

Comprehension

- **True or False**
  1. T   2. F   3. T   4. T   5. F

- **Time Sequence**
  4, 6, 1, 5, 3, 7, 2

Language Skills

- **Structure Practice: Time Signals**
  Answers will vary. Encourage students to rewrite the sentences as a short biographical paragraph as well.

- **Same Word—Different Meanings**
  1. looked at
  2. a timepiece, a piece of jewelry that gives the time
  3. a row of workers doing specific tasks in a factory
  4. a transportation company (here, a shipping company)

Follow-up

- **A Closer Look**
  1. c   2. b   3. d   4. d   5. c

- **Let's Talk about It**
  1. by sneaking out and having parties with her friends
  2. There were a lot of factory jobs available that did not require workers to know English.
  3. Possible responses: It was easy because she got a job right away and she made friends who helped her; on the other hand it was difficult because she didn't know the language.
  4. Answers will vary. An office is a nicer environment; she could learn new skills; she got free trips on the ship.
  5. Answers will vary, but will be similar to the answers for #4.
  6. Answers will vary. Possible response: She is happy to be living in her own country with old friends and family, speaking her own language.

- **Thinking about the Story**

  Students can work in small groups to develop answers, and then share responses with the whole group. Encourage them to provide examples from their own experience for their answers.

- **What's Your Story?**

  Alternative topics: Tell whether you would prefer to work in a factory or an office, and why. Develop an LEA based on the Thinking about the Story discussion.

 **My Work Dream**
Ruben Amaro

Discussion Preview

1. Ask students to name a place in America that they think is beautiful. It can be a place they have already seen or one they would like to visit.
2. Ask students what hobbies they have had, in America or their native country. If students don't respond, ask what they do when they have free time at home.

Picture Preview

What is the man in the picture doing? Ask students if they paint or have ever done any painting. Ask how they feel/felt about painting.

Comprehension

- **True or False**

  1. F   2. F   3. T   4. F   5. T   6. F

- **Multiple Choice**

  1. b   2. d   3. a   4. b

Language Skills

- **Word Families**

  1. proud   4. free

  2. beautiful   5. strong

  3. serious   6. Mexican

- **Structure Practice: Prepositions**

  at, of, of, In, for, in, for, about

- **Vocabulary Review**

  hobby, landscapes, nature, serious, dedicate

- **Structure Practice: Auxiliary Verbs**

  1. *would love*   5. did not paint

  2. do not paint   6. do not want

  3. will dedicate   7. will be

  4. will not wait

Follow-up

- **Let's Talk about It**

  1. Possible responses: His work is good enough to sell; people like his pictures; it is something he feels inside; he feels the need to make something.

  2. He plans to learn English well, and then study painting and spend more time painting.

  3. Answers will vary.

  4. Answers will vary. Possible responses: because he is a creative person, because factory work can become boring, because Ruben doesn't like someone else telling him what to do.

  5. Possible responses: The advantages of company work are regular employment and income; the disadvantages are that the work is often not interesting, and someone is always telling you what to do and when to do it.

The advantages of working alone are that you are your own boss and can choose your own projects and hours; the disadvantages are the irregular pay, the lack of benefits, and the necessity always to find new business.

- **What's Your Story?**
  Alternative topics: Tell about your hobby or what you do in your free time. What is your work dream? Is it better to work for a company or to work alone? (Refer to Let's Talk about It #5.)

A Better Life
Rose E.

Discussion Preview

What is it like for people to come to America without any family or friends in America to help them?

Picture Preview

What are the women in this picture doing? Whose children do you think they are taking care of?

Comprehension

- **True or False**
  1. F   2. T   3. F   4. F   5. T   6. T   7. F

- **Time Sequence**
  5, 2, 1, 3, 4

Language Skills

- **Structure Practice:**
  Simple Present and Present Continuous Tense

1. have	4. have
2. am learning	5. am waiting
3. get	6. is taking

- **Structure Practice**
  Answers will vary, based on students' experiences.

Follow-up

- **Let's Talk about It**

  1. to earn money so her family could buy land

  2. Answer will vary based on students' opinions.

  3. She was happy because she had food and soap.

  4. Possible responses: She has a job, friends, food, soap, clothes, and she's learning to read and write.

  5. Possible responses: She gets sick and has to pay the bills; she has no family in America; she cannot fulfill her expectation to send money home to help her family buy land.

- **Thinking about the Story**

  Students can divide into two groups. One group can be students who think Rose made the right choice to come to America. The other group can be students who think she made the wrong choice. Groups can list their reasons and report their reasons to each other.

- **What's Your Story?**

  Alternative topics: Tell about problems you have had adjusting to the weather in the United States. Discuss how employers should treat the people who work for them, even if the work is done in the home.

 **Disappointment**
Martha Manjulowicz

Discussion Preview

Based on your experience, describe how people in America feel about people from other countries, both positive and negative.

Picture Preview

Where do you think the man in the picture is going? How do you think he feels? What do you think has happened to him?

Comprehension

- **True or False**

  1. T   2. F   3. T   4. F   5. F   6. T

- **Complete the Sentence**

  foreigners, experience, developing, education level, good, clear, accused, switched, bad batch

Language Skills

- **Vocabulary**

  1. accused
  2. blame
  3. disgusted
  4. perseverence
  5. switched
  6. admired

- **Word Families**

  1. education
  2. accusation
  3. admiration
  4. immigration
  5. operation
  6. inspiration
  7. imagination
  8. inflation

- **Structure Practice: Compound Verbs**

  1. They just stay home and collect an unemployment check.
  2. She came to America and looked for an apartment.
  3. He worked during the day and went to school at night.
  4. I studied hard, learned English, worked hard, and got a good job.

Follow-up

- **A Closer Look**

  1. b   2. c   3. b   4. d

- **Let's Talk about It**

  1. because she studied hard, learned English, worked hard, and got a good job
  2. She feels she had no choice; she did what she had to do.
  3. He was accused of doing bad work; he felt people didn't like him; he was very depressed.
  4. According to Martha, sometimes people in America don't like foreigners. She suggests that foreigners are sometimes treated unfairly. This treatment makes them feel hurt and depressed.
  5. Answers will vary.

6. She says that if parents stay home and don't work, children won't learn perseverence or the importance of work. Students' own opinions may vary.

7. Possible responses: Because her husband wasn't working, she had to support her family; she wanted to set a good example for her children.

- **Thinking about the Story**
  Students can work in large or small groups to answer this question. They can list their ideas and put them on the board. Parents can share their ideas and resources for helping their children.

- **What's Your Story?**
  Alternative topic: If students feel comfortable doing so, they can tell about a situation in which they feel they were treated unfairly, and why they think it happened. What effect does a parent's unemployment have on his or her children? (Refer to Let's Talk about It #6.)

14 Helping People
Abreham Hadera

Discussion Preview

1. Discuss the meaning of the word *respect*. Then ask students to list the occupations which are most respected in their native countries. Ask them to talk about why those fields are respected.

2. Ask students who are working if they had the same job in their country. If so, ask what they had to do to reestablish their credentials here. What does a person from outside the United States have to do to continue working in a particular field after coming to America?

Picture Preview

Who do you think the people are in this picture? What do you think they are doing? What might the health care people be talking about?

Comprehension

- **True or False**
  1. F   2. T   3. F   4. F   5. T   6. F

- **Multiple Choice**
  1. b   2. d   3. a   4. b

Language Skills

- **Vocabulary Review**
  Answers will vary.

- **Word Families**

1. examination	5. description
2. injection	6. determination
3. prescription	7. protection
4. donation	8. infection

- **Structure Practice**
  before, During, also, because, After, If

Follow-up

- **A Closer Look**
  1. b   2. a   3. b   4. c   5. a

- **Let's Talk about It**
  1. He gave injections, dressed wounds, did suturing, and distributed tablets for doctors' prescriptions.
  2. Possible responses: He liked it because he was giving assistance to people, because he was happy when some patients were cured, and because the health worker is respected by the community and the patient.
  3. Possible responses: He already knows how to give injections, dress wounds, and do suturing; he knows how to work with doctors and with patients; he has worked with patients under very difficult conditions and with short supplies.
  4. Possible responses: He will have to learn new vocabulary for the medical field, and learn it in a new language; there will be much for him to learn; there will be many tests like the GED to pass; at college he will have to study difficult subjects in a new language; some medical employers might not hire him because he is a black man from a foreign country.

- **What's Your Story?**
  Alternative topic: What do health care workers do in your country and/or in the United States?

15 Being Accepted
Coral Andino

Discussion Preview

1. Why do people sometimes need a change?
2. What training does a nurse need to have? At what places could a nurse find work?

Picture Preview

What is the woman in the picture doing? What might her job be? How do you think the person in the bed feels?

Comprehension

- **True or False**
  1. F   2. F   3. F   4. T   5. F

- **Time Sequence**
  7, 3, 2, 6, 4, 1, 5

- **Complete the Sentence**
  bachelor's degree, popular, bright future, change, nursing boards, nurse's assistant, graduate nurse, orientation, training, graduate, prejudice, passed, impressed, race, color, background

Language Skills

- **Word Families**
  1. perform
  2. supervision
  3. orient
  4. performance
  5. supervise
  6. orientation
  7. supervisor

- **Vocabulary Review**
  Coral worked at a home for the elderly, a small hospital, and Mt. Sinai Hospital. Other possibilities: a clinic, a doctor's office, or a school.

Follow-up

- **Let's Talk about It**

  1. She says she needed a change.

  2. Coral worked as a nurse's assistant in a home for the elderly, a graduate nurse in a small hospital, and a nurse at Mt. Sinai Hospital, a large hospital. At the first, she had a lot of hard work; at the second, she experienced prejudice; at the third, she was not popular, but she learned that love and respect can overcome prejudice and differences of background.

  3. Answers will vary.

  4. She found that the differences among them of race, color, or background no longer got in the way.

- **Thinking about the Story**

  Students can work in pairs or small groups to define what prejudice means to Coral, based on her story. They may also wish to prepare their own definitions of prejudice. After the pairs or small groups develop their own lists of reasons for prejudice, bring the whole group together to compare and discuss the reasons that have been identified.

- **What's Your Story?**

  Alternative topics: Students may wish to develop an LEA on prejudice and can draw on the Thinking about the Story discussion.